I0484449

About the Author

The SAM A. BROWN Entrepreneurial Series serve the Entrepreneur by offering unique advice and tactics in all areas of business. Brown's goal is to build a catalogue of books for you to reference when in need of a strategy or just lack understanding in different facets of your business.

Having successfully built many of his own online businesses and companies, Browns mission is to pay it forward. He believes every aspiring entrepreneur should have access to this information. His approach is to simplify information that can often be overwhelming and seemingly complicated.

If this book was of value to you, please feel free to leave a review on Amazon and share how it helped you, so you too can pay it forward!

More SAM A. BROWN Books

EFFECTIVE EMAIL MARKETING

Table of Contents

Introduction

As a starter, any business needs to know about its core activities in order to determine and evaluate whether the right strategies are being implemented or not. This can be cumbersome if you do not know from where and how to begin. There is nothing to worry about as this can be simply aided by the know-how of basic accounting techniques we present to you in this book – *Accounting Simplified.*

Put simply, accounting is referred to as a financial language that allows you to take a sneak peek into the financial matters of the business. As funds are fundamental to any business, it is the process that enables you to see where the funds are going to and coming from. Having an insight into the incomings and outgoings of funds enables evaluation of the financial performance of the business over a certain time period, as well as the financial position at a given point in time.

To add further, accounting allows you to gauge whether you are allocating and utilizing the funds appropriately or you need to revise the basis for allocation and spending of funds. As it is vital for you to be able to understand the financial activities of your business, it is necessary that you are able to interact with the financial extracts of information. Doing so will facilitate in the evaluation of cash performance, the cash incomings and the cash outgoings.

As a business comprises of multiple assets including cash, accounting helps in the proper recording and maintenance of the business assets. This allows you to determine the overall profit or loss the business has been making as well as to know any drawings made by the owner. Everything is converted into an integrated form with the help of simple accounting techniques and enables you to gain an insight on everything in just a glance.

Accounting also provides useful information for audit and taxation purposes. As your business grows, you will convert it into a company, as it would not remain small forever! And for a company, it is mandatory to have its accounts audited. In order to do that, a proper accounting system is a must. In addition to this, whether you are small or big, you have to file your yearly taxes and the tax authorities are likely to accept your tax return quickly if they are backed up by a proper set of accounts.

Having said this, let us now consider the accounting haves in order to get a grip on the right track!

Chapter 1: Business Essentials

When you start a business and are headed towards success, you need to have an open and positive mind that welcomes innovation and new ideas. It is a must have as without something as fundamental as an open mind, you are unsure of moving forward. This is because imagination holds a place no other thing holds in regards to success. It provides a differentiated approach and unique ideas leading to the provision of a unique service that is hard to beat. Not only this, but an open mind must also be willing to accept various sorts of methods which help a thriving business reach a stable position. This paves way for the fact that imagination and an open mind are more important than knowledge. Therefore imagining yourself successful will ultimately bring you success.

Now that you have an open mind to all the success related ideas, you should create a plan for your business. The plan allows you to accurately define the purpose and goals of your business for the short and long run. Having a plan allows you to strategize everything and then act on it. With the help of plan, you move in a definite direction with a clear focus on the ultimate objectives. Furthermore, the plan will determine what success means to you, therefore you will know where you want your business to head to.

After having a determined plan, you need to have a proper filing system. This means that you should have a system that is transparent and responsive with a proper set of files for individual accounts. Do not take it to be anything complex – it is as simple as clubbing similar documents together into a file!

Then, you should have books of accounts. These may be physical or electronic and can range from off the shelf packages available in the market to using spreadsheets – it entirely depends on your preferences whether you want to stick to simple spreadsheet programs or want to opt for different software packages so as to get benefit from the various sorts of technologies available – alternatively, you may choose the plain old paper but that is considered old fashioned!

Accept different sorts of technologies available as it would allow you to keep up with times. Ignoring new technology can make you lack behind others and your thriving business can soon come to a halt! These include a good hardware platform, such as a latest computer with a quad-core processor, an ample storage space, a good mailing program, a project tracking software, task trackers and to-do lists and an apt accountancy platform. Therefore, consider all the possibilities and do not forget that you need a clear counter and a suitable place to carry out all the tasks. A clear counter without all the mish-mash and the riff-raff is very important in order to soothe the work load for you and allow you to manage things properly, timely and concisely.

And last but not least, you must take out dedicated time for your accountancy tasks. While you would be doing some of them during the course of your business activities, other tasks described later do require some extra time.

Chapter 2: Accounting Essentials

Before heading on towards having a simplified accounting system which will help you in excelling your business and enable you to catch up in the race, you need to have a basic knowledge of accounting essentials- that is a must!

These essentials pertain to allow you to record periodic transactions while keeping in view the dual effect. This entails that you know about the things that make up any business, large or small. These are the assets, liabilities and capital. Though a business is made up of these three elements, it is important to remember that assets move in the opposite direction of liabilities and capital, thereby you can club liabilities and capital together which fall in the same class. It is worth noting that all these items stay in the business in the long run. What differs from one period to another is income and expenditure.

Once you know about the basic elements that make up a business, you must then understand that one transaction has two effects. An increase in one thing leads to a decrease in another, or vice versa. For instance, if a customer pays you, you receive cash. This means that cash increases and the receivable decreases. This can also be interpreted in a manner that an increase in cash leads to an increase in sales (as it is opposite in nature, the increase in sales records the dual effect).

Whether it is an asset, a liability or capital, we use accounts to record each of these items. Regardless of the account type, every account is defined by a debit and a credit. Since accounts have been on paper in the form of letter T, to write something on the left side of the account is known as a Debit entry and to write something on the right side of the account is known as a Credit entry.

When you wish to increase an asset, you debit the account and when you wish to decrease the asset, you credit the account. The opposite is true for liabilities and capital. As this is an equation, and since assets in the business must be equal at any point to the equity plus liabilities, this must mean that the total debits at the point in time must equal the total credits.

When your expenses in the daily course of business increase, you debit the relevant account head and when the expenses decrease, you credit the account. When you earn and have to record your income, you credit the account and a decrease in the income is recorded as a debit entry.

This dual effect lies at the heart of an accounting system and enables in gaining an understanding of the ongoing scenario. Had it not been the proper recording of the routine transactions with a coherent record of how it affects other parts of the business, there would have been so much chaos and the time which needed to be allocated to the business would have been wasted on unimportant activities. Once you understand how one thing is affecting the other parts of business and to what extent, you can easily plan out strategies that enable insight and successful planning.

This understanding is further simplified by the existence of accounting journals that may be electronic or physical. What type you use is highly dependent on your preference. These accounting journals are known as books of prime entry or books of original entry. You will use these books to prepare financial statements later. This is because if the accounts were to be updated every time a transaction took place, there is a high chance that errors would be made and a lot of time would be consumed entering many small entries. Books of prime entry exist to make the process easy and so that you can avoid the clutter. When a transaction occurs, it is recorded in a book of prime entry that is just a simple recording of the transaction with the details of the amount, customer or supplier and the date. Put simply, it is an extensive list of the routine transitions.

There are different books of prime entry that record different types of transactions. These books of prime entry and the transactions they record are as follows:

- Sales day book
  - Transaction type: Credit sales
- Purchases day book
  - Transaction type: Credit purchases
- Sales returns day book
  - Transaction type: Returns of goods sold on credit
- Purchases returns day book
  - Transaction type: Returns of goods bought on credit
- Cash book
  - Transaction type: All bank transactions
- Petty cash book
  - Transaction type: Cash in hand transactions
- The journal
  - Transactions not recorded anywhere else

Chapter 3: Understanding the Sales Day Book

Sales day book, also known as sales journal is used to record all the sales made on credit. The figures posted in the sales day book relate to each individual sale made regarding the credit sales of goods for the concerned period. Depending upon how much your sales are, you might decide to close your journal daily, weekly or monthly. Whenever you choose to do so, your entry will remain the same.

You may draw up a simple sales day book using either a four column or a six column approach, depending upon whether or not you wish to account for sales tax. If you do not record sales tax, then use the three column sales day book. An example of the journal is produced below.

Sales Day Book			
Date	Invoice Number	Description	Amount ($)

If you decide to record the tax, the following type of journal will be required.

Sales Day Book				
Date	Description	Amount Exclusive of Sales Tax ($)	Tax Amount	Amount Inclusive of Sales Tax ($)

Here are your instructions:

For every day when you make credit sales, just enter the name of the person and the amount he or she has to pay. As the day/week/month draws to an end, you total the amount column and carry out one entry with the total instead of several different entries.

You should allot a book or a spreadsheet with one page per customer to keep their record in a statement form. This would tell you how much your customers owe and needs to be tied in with the receivables account explained below.

Receivables can be explained as a debit balance that is due from the customers in total. The sales day book records the balance of each individual customer and totals them, which is then credited to the sales account. This resulting figure that is posted to the sales account is the receivables balance as receivables is the total amount you still have to receive from your customers.

When a sale is made, it is recorded in the sales day book. The customers in the sales day book are debited with the amount pertaining to them. At the end of the period, the total is posted to the sales account on the credit side. The double entry is accordingly completed.

Entry for a sale on credit:

Debit Receivables

Credit Sales

When cash is received, the following entry is passed:

Debit Cash

Credit Receivables

The debit and credit against the receivables consequently cancel out each other and the double entry that remains can be simplified to:

Debit Cash

Credit Sales

You will be pleased to know that you can speed up the receipt process from your customers by offering them cash discounts. This will, however, affect the double entries you will make but stay calm! This is not something to worry about and is very simple to deal with.

When you give discount to your customers, you record it as:

Debit Discount Allowed

Credit Receivables

Therefore, the cash you receive will be the total amount less the discount allowed.

Chapter 4: Understanding the Purchases Day Book

Purchases day book is also known as purchases journal and is used for the recording of all sorts of purchases made on credit. The figures which are posted in the purchases day book relate to each individual purchase made regarding the credit purchase of goods for the related period. Depending on the nature and extent of purchases, you might decide to close your purchases journal on a daily, weekly or monthly basis. Whatever the period you choose, the entry will remain the same.

Similar to the sales day book, you may draw up a purchases day book using either a four column or a six column approach. This is dependent upon whether or not you wish to record the input sales tax. If you do not wish to record the input sales tax, use the three column purchase day book. An example of the journal is produced below.

Purchases Day Book			
Date	Invoice Number	Description	Amount ($)

If you have decided to know the tax rate concerning each purchase and want to know the tax exclusive and tax inclusive amount, the following journal will be required.

Purchases Day Book				
Date	Description	Amount Exclusive of Sales Tax ($)	Tax Amount	Amount Inclusive of Sales Tax ($)

Here are your instructions:

For every day when you make credit purchases, just enter the name of the person you purchased goods from and the amount he or she has to pay. As the day/week/month draws to an end, you total the amount column and carry out one entry with the total in place of several different entries.

Next, in order to keep the supplier's record in a statement form, allot a book or a spreadsheet file with one page per supplier to know how much you owe to each of your suppliers. These individual amounts will be tied with the payables account explained below.

Payables balance is a credit balance that is explained as the balance due to the suppliers in total. The purchases day book documents the balance of each individual supplier and totals them, which is then debited to the purchases account. This resulting figure is posted to the purchases account as the payables balance that is the amount due to your suppliers and needs to be paid.

When a purchase is made, it is recorded in the purchases day book. The suppliers in the purchases day book are credit with the amount due to them. When the period ends, the total is transferred to the purchases account on the debit side. You see the double entry has been completed.

Explaining the purchase on credit, the following entries are made:

Debit Purchases

Credit Payables

When cash is paid, the following entry is made:

Debit Payables

Credit Cash

It can be seen that the debit and credit against the payables cancel each other out, and the double entry in essence is:

Debit Purchases

Credit Cash

Chapter 5: Understanding the Sales Returns Day Book

Sales returns day book is a book of prime entry that records the returns of goods from customers. You must note that you will have customers who might want to return the goods they have purchased. There is also a possibility that the goods you have sold might be faulty and thus, you must be prudent enough to provide for this possibility.

Like the sales day book, a sales returns day book also can be prepared in the four or six column approach. Whatever the format, this depends on your preferences. Examples of the sales returns day book with and without tax are given below.

Sales Returns Day Book

Date	Invoice Number	Description	Amount ($)

Sales Returns Day Book

Date	Description	Amount Exclusive of Sales Tax ($)	Tax Amount	Amount Inclusive of Sales Tax ($)

Chapter 6: Purchases Returns Day Book

As your customers would like to return some of the goods to you, in the same way you would like to return some of the goods to your suppliers. This would be because you might have agreed terms with the suppliers that any unsold goods would be returned to them or simply because the goods have turned out to be defective. This return of goods is records in the purchases return day book. This recording enables you to be able to adjust your stock in accordance with the actual purchases minus those returned to the suppliers.

Like the purchases day book, a purchases return journal can be in made into four or six column depending on whether you want to account for tax separately or not. Examples of the purchases returns day book with and without tax are given below.

Purchases Returns Day Book			
Date	Invoice Number	Description	Amount ($)

Purchases Returns Day Book				
Date	Description	Amount Exclusive of Sales Tax ($)	Tax Amount	Amount Inclusive of Sales Tax ($)

Chapter 7: The Cash Book and Petty Cash Book

Cash book pertains to be a financial journal that records all the receipts and payments which normally go into your bank. For example, receipts from customers are recorded here, cash sale takings are recorded here and if you have invested any money in a deposit account or with a building society, its interest also lands here. A cash book lies at the heart of the financial bookkeeping. This is because cash is fundamental to the operations of any business and the most liquid asset that helps in the day to day operations. The cash book is then reconciled after a specific period with the bank statements.

Cash book helps in the management of cash on a regular basis and allows you to see where the cash is coming from and going to. It simplifies the difficult business processes and creates ease for you.

When you record a receipt in the cash book, the entries are as follows.

To record a cash sale:

Debit Cash

Credit Sales

To record receipt from a customer:

Debit Cash

Credit Receivables

To record a payment to a supplier in cash:

Debit Payables

Credit Cash

To record a cash purchase:

Debit Purchases

Credit Cash

The cash book, at the period end, not only helps in ascertaining income and expenses, but also helps gauge expenses and provides the cash available to the business at that point in time.

Petty Cash Book

This is an extension of the cash book, which is kept to record the movement of cash in hand. As the name suggests, the cash in hand is small or "petty" and is used to record small expenses like those for postage stamps, local fares, tea and coffee etc.

Chapter 8: The Journal

The journal is a special book used to record different types of entries that are beyond the scope of the journals mentioned above. It is used to record entries such as:

- The purchase and sale of fixed assets (cars, buildings, machinery, fixtures and fittings, computers, etc)
- Contra entries (between the accounts of a person who happens to be a customer as well as a supplier of a business)
- To pass correcting entries (in case a mistake has been made)

Chapter 9: A Simple Example, Practically Illustrated

Let us now consider the example of ABC Ltd. that started with a capital of $10,000 and traded for the month of January as follows.

It made the following sales on credit.

Sales Day Book			
Date	Description	invoice no	Amount
01-Jan-15	P john	0001	324
12-Jan-15	D Watson	0002	345
24-Jan-15	E Schultz	0003	700
28-Jan-15	D Brown	0004	830
30-Jan-15	J Kelly	0005	750
	Total		2949

During January, the following customers returned goods.

Sales Returns Day Book			
Date	Description	Credit Note No	Amount
26-Jan-15	E Schultz	0001	200
31-Jan-15	D Brown	0002	130
	Total		330

The following credit purchases were made for the first month of trading.

Purchases Day Book			
Date	Description	invoice no	Amount
03-Jan-15	Paul & Co	1272	120
12-Jan-15	Matt & Co	7550	240
19-Jan-15	Office Supplies Ltd	8135	670
24-Jan-15	The Paper Mart	KTJ 132	220
29-Jan-15	Brownie and Sons	OF-0001-X	775
	Total		2025

The following goods were returned to suppliers.

Purchases Returns Day Book			
Date	Description	Debit Note No	Amount
21-Jan-15	Office Supplies	0001	100
28-Jan-15	The Paper Mart	0002	50
	Total		150

The cash position of the business is evident from the cash book. Cash came into the business and out of the business as follows.

Cash Book					
Cash Receipts			Cash Payments		
Date	Description	Amount	Date	Description	Amou
01-Jan-15	Opening balance	10,000	05-Jan-15	Paul & Co	
01-Jan-15	Sales	1200	14-Jan-15	Matt & Co	
05-Jan-15	Sales	1500	17-Jan-15	Rent	1
08-Jan-15	P John	324	18-Jan-15	Electricity	
14-Jan-15	D Watson	345	21-Jan-15	Office Supplies Ltd	
15-Jan-15	sales	1200	28-Jan-15	The Paper Mart	
29-Jan-15	D Brown	400	29-Jan-15	Wages and Salaries	1
31-Jan-15	J kelly	200	31-Jan-15	Telephone and internet	
	Total Receipts	15,169		**Total Payments**	4
	Cash remaining	**10,689**			

It's time to use this data to find out your profit and loss. For this, a simple profit and loss statement is prepared in order to know whether the business is earning a profit or operating at a loss for the period under consideration and allows considerable insight into the income and expenditures your business is incurring.

Profit And Loss Statement

Sales:	
Cash Sales	3900
Credit Sales	2949
Total Sales	6849
Less Sales Returns	330
Net Sales	6519
Cost of Goods Sold:	
Purchases	2025
Less Purchase returns	150
Net Purchases	1875
Gross Profit	4644
Less expenses:	
Rent	1000
Electricity	500
Wages And Salaries	1500
Telehpone and internet	600
Total Expenses	3600
Profit /(Loss)	1044

It is important for you to take care of the following points:

Total all the cash sales from the cash book and enter it into the profit and loss account.

Total all the credit sales from the sales day book and enter it into the profit and loss account.

Total all the sales return from the sales return day book and enter it into the profit and loss.

Likewise, total all the credit purchases from the purchases day book and enter into the profit and loss account.

Total all the purchases returns from the purchases returns day book and enter into the profit and loss account.

You can tell the figures from the highlighted colors as illustrated, in order to know where they come from.

Now, in order to know the position of business at any point in time, you need to have a balance sheet. A balance is nothing more than a snapshot of a business's assets, liabilities and capital. Taking our example further, the balance sheet is illustrated as follows.

Balance Sheet as at 31 January 2015

Assets	$
Cash	10,689
Receivables	1350
Total Assets	**12,039**
Capital	
Opening Balance	10000
Add Profit	1044
	11044
Liabilities	
Payables	995
Total Capital and Liabilities	**12039**

A balance sheet is composed of assets, liabilities and capital. The cash position is apparent from the cash book, and the balance is taken from the cash book.

The receivables balance is the total of net customer balances that can also be made into a list of receivables balances to make things simple. The position of receivables in our example is as under.

Customers Balances

	P John		Debit	Credit	Balance
Date	Description		Debit	Credit	Balance
01-Jan-15	Sales		324		324
08-Jan-15	Cash			324	0

	D Watson		Debit	Credit	Balance
Date	Description		Debit	Credit	Balance
12-Jan-15	Sales		345		345
14-Jan-15	Cash			345	0

	E Schultz		Debit	Credit	Balance
Date	Description		Debit	Credit	Balance
24-Jan-15	Sales		700		700
26-Jan-15	Sales Returns			200	500

	D Brown		Debit	Credit	Balance
Date	Description		Debit	Credit	Balance
28-Jan-15	Sales		830		830
29-Jan-15	Cash			400	430
31-Jan-15	Sales Returns			130	300

	J Kelly		Debit	Credit	Balance
Date	Description		Debit	Credit	Balance
30-Jan-15	Sales		750		750
31-Jan-15	Cash			200	550

The list of balances to simplify all of this looks like as:

Customer	Amount ($)
P John	0
D Watson	0
E Schultz	500
D Brown	300
J Kelly	550
Total	**1350**

The capital consists of the opening balance first. Please remember that:

- Profit increases capital whenever it is earned
- Loss decreases capital whenever it is incurred
- Drawings by the owner decrease the capital as funds move out.

Since we have a profit here, it is added to the opening balance to get the closing balance for January. Then come the liabilities, the amounts that we have to pay to our suppliers. The total amount that we have to pay to our suppliers is the net of supplier balances that can also be made into a list of payables balances, just like the receivables balances. The position of payables in our example is as under.

Suppliers Balances

	Paul & Co			
Date	Description	Debit	Credit	Balance
03-Jan-15	Purchases		120	-120
08-Jan-15	Cash	120		0

	Matt & Co			
Date	Description	Debit	Credit	Balance
12-Jan-15	Purchases		240	-240
14-Jan-15	Cash	240		0

	Office Supplies Ltd			
Date	Description	Debit	Credit	Balance
19-Jan-15	Purchases		670	-670
21-Jan-15	Purchase Returns	100	0	-570
21-Jan-15	Cash	350		-220

	The Paper Mart			
Date	Description	Debit	Credit	Balance
24-Jan-15	Purchases		220	-220
28-Jan-15	Purchase Returns	50		-170
28-Jan-15	Cash	170		0

	Brownie & Sons			
Date	Description	Debit	Credit	Balance
29-Jan-15	Purchases		775	-775
				-775

The negative balance is indicative of the fact that you owe your suppliers and need to pay them. Simplifying the suppliers into a list of balances, it will appear as follows.

Supplier	Amount ($)

Paul & Co	0
Matt & Co	0
Office Supplies	220
The Paper Mart	0
Brownie & Sons	775
Total	**995**

Chapter 10: Business Growth Ensured

Concluding the importance of accounting for your business, it is a must in order to strive in the right direction. Though without accounting you might think you are doing the things right, you can never know how well you are performing unless and until you have an integrated approach which can provide a snapshot of different things in relation to each other.

Had it not been accounting, you would have never been able to spot out the problems concerning your business. Now, let us suppose that your business had been overspending and you are worried about where the things have been going wrong? What is it that needs to be addressed in order to manage the things accordingly and set them on the right path? How would you know where the problem lies? Is it the cash, other assets or expenses from where the problem is arising?

In order to get things right and allow you to see a snapshot, simple accounting techniques can be applied which not only help you sort out these problems but also help you to keep things in an integrated and uncluttered form. The journals described previously do the job for you, leaving you with less stress and a lot of ease. You can precisely use them for your advantage and gauge various things at the same time.

Moreover, it is crucial that you know how efficient are your operations. This is because unless and until a business is efficient, it cannot thrive and compete with other businesses. This helps in planning a course of action that needs to be taken according to the situation and take the business decisions. These can collectively help your business to grow and assist you in taking a glimpse of what is going on. Taking a look at what the business has and how much it has earned or its capacity to earn allows a sneak peek into the functionality of the business.

Not only this, but you can keep accurate records of the company's assets, liabilities, capital, expenses and income. This will enable an insight into whether you can carry out the normal business operations and whether any area needs more cash, investment and whether the business is generating enough income to cover the running expenses as well as to sustain for the foreseeable future.

You can also analyze trends of sales, purchases, returns, behavior of assets and cash that allows you to review each area individually and helps you keep track. Without an accounting system, this is not possible and you can easily deviate from your objectives.

As a business is a mix of different functions, like purchasing, sales, marketing and human resources, accounting enables you to take a quick look on the different aspects as to how these functions operate. When you know how each function of the business is operating, you can allocate costs in a better manner and take the decisions with a greater insight.

Also, keeping track of the financial information is the best thing that keeps you up to date with the business and thus, you interact with it on a regular and timely basis. Remember, like any other thing, your business needs your time and consideration so it can flourish and if you befriend it, it can provide you with satisfactory returns with the right amount of hard work!

Effective Email Marketing by Sam A. Brown

If *Accounting Simplified* has helped you and your business in any way, than you might like Sam A. Browns other book *Effective Email Marketing*. We have enclosed the first two chapters of his book for you to sample. If you want more you will find the link at the end of this preview. Enjoy!

Introduction

Making the decision to tap into the marketing powers of email marketing in your business is a profitable one. While the internet rapidly changes, email has been one of few platforms that have stood the test of the volatile nature of the internet.

With snail mail delivery being the miracle of the twentieth century, email is the miracle of the twenty-first century. One of the best things about the human condition is that we are ever evolving and improving. We can get things done much more efficiently and effectively than ever before.

As individuals, it is so important that we are utilizing the tools that have evolved for us to their most advantageous usage. To do this, we must remain educated and motivated to evolve with technology.

The first thing that most people learn to do when they first sit in front of a computer is to send and receive email. There are a lot of people that think that if they can send and receive email, they are computer literate.

Chapter 1: What can Email Marketing do for your Business?

Email allows people instant access to communication. Marketers love instant access and communication is a marketers' lifeblood. The marriage was inevitable.

The marriage of email and marketing has had a long and healthy relationship. It hasn't, however, been without its problems. There are those who have abused the relationship and caused it pain and suffering. There were just too many marketing emails that were sent too often and personal computer users objected to opening their beloved email programs only to find them flooded with advertising, some of which was a bit 'lacking in taste' to put it mildly.

Even though this book is on email marketing, you need to come to terms with some truths about it.

Gmail, one of the leading email providers, has recently implemented the 'priority markers' feature allowing their users to mark selected emails as important and thus change the ways people prioritize their emails for reading consumption every time they check their Inbox. And let's be honest: promotional emails rarely ever reach PRIORITY status!

Then they implement a smart system that detects and filters spam emails and it gets tweaked frequently, therefore making even legit email marketing harder.

It is for these reasons that EFFECTIVE Email Marketing is more important than ever. With strategy and marketing smarts, you can actually make your customers WANT to receive your emails and draw them into taking further action within the spectrum of your brand.

You need to understand that there will always be new technology, and technology changes things. The thing that separates successful businesses apart from the rest, is that they stay on top of these technology trends and market themselves accordingly.

So what do these technology trends mean for email marketing? Is it dated? Will it work? The beautiful thing about emails is that they have endured many ebbs and currents of the fast-paced world of technology. While we have seen other mediums come and go (Ahem, MySpace), email has and will be here for the long haul. What has (and will continue to) change in emails is the way our customers use and interact with them.

This means you need to employ different, more effective tactics to capture your prospect's attention and get him to act on YOUR email instead of your competitors!

This is imperative especially if you happen to operate in a niche that is highly competitive, and that it is not uncommon for people to subscribe to more than one mailing lists – examples like, health, real estate, fashion, swimwear, tourism ect.

In other words, for almost every subscriber who joins your mailing list you can safely assume that they are also on your competitor's mailing lists.

There is also the issue of 'giving away free content'. While offering your customers value and building your brand up to be an expertise is important you do not want to over-do it on the free stuff for the following reasons:

First of all, it defeats your true purpose and goal of building a mailing list. The reason you build a list is to convert your prospects into buyers, and buyers into long time customers! This is essentially why you are building a list ripe to email market and do it for profits!

Secondly, people don't read a lot when they receive emails. People are time poor in this day and age and often have many emails to go through. They are not going to sit there and read a 400 word email offering them tips and tricks.

Lastly, people (primarily sub-consciously) appreciate things more when they pay for them. Whatever they paid for will increase in value immediately because they actually spent money on it. This is very good news for you! The work is in approaching them effectively to pay money for something that will actually add value to their lives.

Even if you are sending a newsletter or an article you should always hook them in with a product, something of value or a call to action. In this day and age, knowledge is everywhere. You need to provide your email list with something tangible, something that will excite them and something that links back to your brand and bottom line.

Most email marketers reason that giving content is important because it will reduce their un-subscription rates while making their subscribers happy. This is completely false. One, you can never please everyone and it is inevitable that you will get unsubscribers. Two, when people realize they don't have time to read or 'consume' your emails and are not getting something tangible and lasting, they will hit the un-subscribe link at the bottom of the email, thus you still get un-subscriptions!

Don't just take my word for it. Take a look at what leading Internet companies are doing in the area of email marketing.

If you are on Amazon's mailing list or bought something from them before, notice that Amazon.com always sends promotional email offers recommending other products related to your previous purchase? They do not give free tips. They do not give 'how tos' and they certainly don't give free content. They are in business of selling you more stuff, and that's coming from an Internet company that 34 billion dollars a year in revenue!

Groupon.com always send bulks of discount offers in their emails. But they never give free content. It's always been promotional emails all the way!

These are just prime examples. Subscribe to the list of any big companies and you will see they always send out email offers; not free content!

Forget about trying to please everyone with 'free content' – the true purpose of email marketing is to simply convert as many prospects into buyers as possible. Period.

If you already have a list of buyers, your next goal is to get them to become lifetime customers, happy with your product and excited about what your brand has to offer. If they want reading material they will follow a blog.

www.ingramcontent.com/pod-product-compliance
Lightning Source LLC
Chambersburg PA
CBHW070758180526
45168CB00004B/1658